PRISON SLANG

CW00545700

Abson Books London
First published June 2005
Cover design Chris Bird

Printed by Gutenberg Press, Malta
ISBN 0 902920898

PRISON SLANG

compiled by Peter Mann

ABSON BOOKS LONDON
5 Sidney Square London E1 2EY
Tel 020 7790 4737 Fax 020 7790 7346
email absonbooks@aol.com | web www.absonbooks.co.uk

PREFACE

This book of *porridge* parlance has been compiled from personal experience – the author having served nearly two decades as a guest of Her Majesty.

It gives the history behind such words as *slopping out* and *screw* while providing much information on modern terms, revealing the reason why being taken down the *block* by the *Gestapo* and given the *black pill* or *liquid cosh* should be avoided at all costs

Slang of any derivation is peculiar to its locality and a compilation can never be definitive. Prison Slang is composed of words most commonly used in UK prisons

Enjoy it but make sure you never have to use it for real.

A

'A' cat   top security prisoner
AG   Assistant Governor
AVs   accumulated visits
ant killer   powder put on floor and behind pipes to kill off cockroaches
arse licker   prisoner who has put himself out to get good reports
association   recreation period
attah   Pakistani name for class A drugs

B

'B' cat   high security prisoner
BOV   Board of Visitors (body of magistrates which listens to prisoners' complaints)
bacon   sex offender
bacon bonce   sex offender (see nonce)

bag	small quantity of heroin
bagheads	heroin users and dealers
bagel	wrap of heroin worth £10
bandsman	escapee who wears suit with yellow stripes running down the trousers
banged up	locked up in a cell
baron	prisoner who lends out tobacco for a profit
barricading up	using cell furniture to block up a door
basic	lowest behavioural category
bashing	beating up
beast	sex offender
bender	suspended sentence handed out on a governor's adjudication
bent screw	dishonest officer
bib	yellow or orange bib worn by prisoners when on social visits

bib and brace	body belt used to control unruly prisoner (put around prisoner's waist with hands placed in steel cuffs)
Bill and Bens	prison garden workers
birch	form of punishment last used in Hull Prison in 1962
biscuit	ecstasy tablet
black pill	kick in the arse from a prison officer.
blade	knife (made in prison workshop)
bleat	petition the Home Secretary
block	segregation unit
blue band	trustee (with more trust than a **red band**)
bluey	black man
board	interview for parole etc
body bags	senior female officers
boom box	powerful music system

boss	prison officer
bridge	small structure spanning either side of wing walkways, usually reserved for officers as a controlling point
brief	solicitor
brownie points	see **arse licker**
bruv	friend
bully beef	chief officer
burglars	security officers
buzz	rumour
buzzer	emergency bell in prisoner's cell

C

'C' cat	intermediate security prisoner
CVs	compassionate visits
CT	corrective training (no longer in use)

cage	cell, usually in the segregation unit
card	phone card (can be used as collateral)
cardboard gangster	prisoner who struts around like John Wayne
caser	officer always reporting prisoners
centre	main controlling point of the prison
charlie's heroes	informers
chief	most senior officer (no longer in use)
chive	weapon: knife, razor blade
chokey	bread and water (now known as the segregation unit)
clothesliner	derogatory name for petty criminal (originally someone who stole washing)
cocktail	mixture of drugs used to keep unruly prisoners quiet
coir mat	cell mat made from rope
con	prisoner (short for convict)

cooper's troopers	psychiatric patients (named after a Dr Cooper at Parkhurst Prison whose patients had psychiatric problems)
core	sexual offender treatment programme
corner shop	prisoner who can access any form of contraband, such as drugs, porn magazines etc
country, the	Dartmoor Prison
cowboy hat	cardboard chamber pot used in segregation unit
cut up	use a knife or razor blade to wound a prisoner's face

D

'D' cat	lowest security prisoner (in open conditions)
DC	detention centre
DLP	Discretionary Lifers' Panel
dabs	fingerprints

darbies	handcuffs
debtor's disease	going sick to avoid **barons**
dep	deputy governor
deps	short for depositions, legal papers or sworn evidence
depth charge	prison puddings
Desperate Dan pie	meat and potato pie: the same shape, size and weight as a normal house brick and just as heavy
diesel	tea
dip	place where prison officers pick up mail, notices and application forms
dip test	passing urine to be tested for drugs
dirty dishes	false evidence
dirty protest	to throw excreta over cell walls as a form of protest

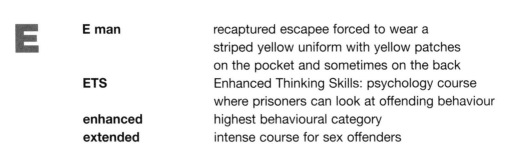

doing a runner	escaping from custody
doing bird	on a prison sentence
dorm	a large cell shared by up to ten prisoners
Dot Cotton	elderly female prison officer
double cuffed	prisoner handcuffed to an officer with two sets of handcuffs
dry bath	searched when naked

E

E man	recaptured escapee forced to wear a striped yellow uniform with yellow patches on the pocket and sometimes on the back
ETS	Enhanced Thinking Skills: psychology course where prisoners can look at offending behaviour
enhanced	highest behavioural category
extended	intense course for sex offenders

F

Fick un	hand rolled cigarette – fat
Fingers in the door	a cell thief who, when caught, has his fingers crushed in cell door
Fin un	hand rolled cigarette – thin
five fingered widow	masturbation
flag	cell indicator
forty-threes	prisoners placed on protection
fraggle	prisoner who has psychiatric problems
free flow	freedom of movement to and from prisoner's place of work
full moon	twelve month prison sentence

G

GOAD	Good Order And Discipline; prisoner who is segregated from others (usually a subversive)
Gabriel	chapel organiser
ganja	marijuana

gash	anything which is spare to requirement
gate fever	getting near to release date
Gestapo	officers who style themselves on the Nazi SS – slashed peaks on caps, hobnailed boots and aggressive manner
ghosted out	prisoner suddenly moved without warning (usually a subversive)
god squad	prisoners who attend church regularly, usually to get parole
god's commandos	ditto
Googie Withers	female governor (from actress who starred in TV series *Within These Walls*)
granddad shirt	old style blue-and-white striped shirt coveted by prisoners
grapevine	underground communication
grass, a	informer

green band	trustee (with more trust then a **red band** or a **blue band**)
grey bwai	black man's name for a white man (bwai = boy)
griff	finding out information
gruel	stew made from the previous day's leftovers

hair cut	short sentence
half moon	six month prison sentence
handful	five year prison sentence
hobbit	prisoner who obeys the system without argument
hobbit hole	place that hobbits frequent (e.g. the television room)
hooch	illegal alcohol brew
hotplate hamster	prison officer who hovers around food serving area waiting for leftovers
housewife	bag containing needles, cotton and thimble

15

I

IPVs	Inter Prison Visits, usually from relatives
IMB	Independent Monitoring Board (body of magistrates who listens to prisoners' complaints – the new name for Board of Visitors)

J

jam roll	parole
joey	officer who runs errands
John Wayne	see **cardboard gangster**
judas hole	spy hole; aperture in cell door
jugged	to have hot water thrown over a prisoner (usually a grass or sex offender)
jumping through hoops	to do offending behaviour courses only to get parole

K

kanga	prison officer
kangaroo	screw (prison officer)
kangaroo court	group of prisoners making judgement on another prisoner (usually a sex offender)
kennel	cell

L

LBBs	lights, bolts and bars (daily check)
LDV	Lifer Day Visits; day set aside for lifers and lifers' families
lag	recidivist; prisoner who has served many sentences
lagging	prison sentence of more than a year
landings	accommodation floor level
leg	spur or landing on a closed wing
letterbox	see judas hole
lie down	prisoner who is moved to another prison for 28 days, usually for being subversive

liquid cosh	calming drug injected into unruly prisoner in order to subdue and control
listener	sympathetic prisoner who listens to other's problems
lock down	when every prisoner in the prison is locked up

M

MDT	Mandatory Drug Test (normally once a year)
magic wand	hand-held metal detector used for body searches
married quarters	wing, or part of a wing, used to accommodate homosexuals
Mars Bar	scar
merchandise	illegal goods
merry-go-round	prisoner who is moved from prison to prison as punishment for major misdemeanours

monster	sex offender
Moss Side	welsh rarebit, particular to Strangeways
mufti	riot squad
mug shot	head-and-shoulders photograph taken for records
muppets	half-wits, fools, idiots

N

nicked	placed on report
night clockie	night patrol officer
night stand	prisoner who is allowed to leave his cell between the hours of 10pm and 6am (only in prisons with electrically operated doors)
No.1	number one governor
noddy suit	coloured prison tracksuit
nonce	sex offender (abbreviation of Not Of Normal Criminal Element)

nosey	censor of letters
numbers	on protection (usually for sex offenders), *e.g. don't talk to him, he's on the numbers*
nutter	prisoner with a mental or social problem

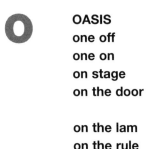

OASIS	Offender Assessment System
one off	prisoner taken off the workshop role
one on	prisoner added to the workshop role
on stage	extra privileges earned (no longer officially in use)
on the door	kicking and banging on a cell door, usually in protest
on the lam	on the run from the police or prison (mainly US)
on the rule	prisoners under protection (usually sex offenders)

on tour	see **merry-go-round**	
one flew over the		
cuckoo's nest	prisoner transferred to Broadmoor lunatic asylum	
over the wall	to escape from prison	

PD	Preventative Detention (no longer in use)
PP9'd	Beaten with a PP9 battery in a sock
pad	cell
paedopumps	blue/white canvas gym shoes worn only by alleged sex offenders
page 16	prisoners' wing behaviour report
panic button	general alarm bell
pat down	an officer patting a prisoner's body to find if contraband is hidden on his person
patches	see **E man**

peep hole	see **judas hole**
penthouse suite	top floor cell
peter	cell (peter = safe)
peterman	safecracker, safe-blower
pigeonholes	small box-like alcoves where information is left for officers
pinion apparatus	see **bib and brace**
pinioned	hands held in a body belt around prisoner's waist
pipe	tube, usually a biro pen casing, used to smoke marijuana
plastic gangster	see **cardboard gangster**
porridge	doing time (sentence)
powder	quantity of cocaine
prison solicitor	educated, legal-minded, helpful prisoner
prison telephone	talking to another prisoner by using the toilet as a means of communication

private spends	money sent in by friends and relatives to top up prison earnings
puff	see powder
put the bubble in	inform on another prisoner

Q

quack	prison doctor
Quasimodo	chapel orderly

R

R & R	Reasoning and Rehabilitation – see ETS (not to be confused with rest and recuperation)
rat	prison officer who is much disliked by prisoners
recess	area set aside within accommodation blocks to dispose of waste
red band	trustee

resettlement prison	prison that caters for long-term/lifer prisoners, preparing them for release into the community
room service	cell bell used to call an officer (usually pressed out of devilment)
round robin	secret petition circulated by prisoners
rub down	officer rubbing a prisoner's body to find hidden contraband (see also **pat down**)
rubber socks	condoms supplied to homosexuals by the Health Care Centre

S

SOTP	Sexual Offenders Treatment Programme
scooby doo	prison officer
score	to acquire illegal substances, e.g. drugs or alcohol
scran	food

scran's up	meals ready for serving
screw	prison officer (the name deriving from when convicts had to turn a crank as punishment, and when a screw became loose the convict cried out *'Screw!'* in order for an officer to tighten it)
screw driver	chief officer or principle officer
seg	segregation unit
separates	cells in the segregation unit that are put aside for prisoners under Rule 43 (segregation of sex offenders)
seven days all round	seven days' punishment handed out on an adjudication (no association, no wages, no television and no private spends)
shanghaicd	suddenly shipped out of prison

shitting up	throwing excreta over staff
silent cell	padded cell in segregation unit, also found in the hospital wing
sit down	ask to leave workplace to defecate
skins	cigarette papers
sky pilot	prison chaplin
slippery	prisoner who wangles his way out of any situation; crafty, devious
slopping out	disposing of waste from the previous night into a latrine in recess (still happening in some prisons)
smashing up	destroying cell fixtures and fittings
sniffer dogs	dogs, usually cocker spaniels, used to locate drugs in cells and workshops

snout	tobacco (derives from the days of the silent prison system, in which, if a prisoner wanted a cigarette, he would tap his nose – i.e. his snout – to attract the attention of the tobacco baron)
special	cell search (when grassed up)
spin	cell search, usually by two officers
spliff	hand-rolled cigarette containing marijuana
spoon	cell key (at one time cells could be opened by using a spoon)
spring the lock	open a cell door by an officer pressing a small button on the lock (used as a safety measure to stop hostage-taking)
spy hole	see **judas hole**
stage paper	newspaper issued on a daily rotation basis
stand up	ask to leave workplace to urinate

standard	intermediate behavioural category
star	prisoner wearing a red star on his sleeve to denote he is a first offender (no longer in use)
stash	hidden contraband
stiff	note passed over during a social visit, either by a prisoner or a visitor (usually something very important, e.g. a serious complaint, that cannot be said on the phone or in a normal letter)
stinger	electrical appliance used to heat water in a cup (stings when hot)
stir	doing time
stir crazy	suffering from prison psychosis after years behind bars
stitched up	falsely accused by a prison officer
stote the ba'	paedophile/sex offender

straight-goer	non-criminal
strike	matches, or a piece of matchbox used to strike matches against, e.g. *have you got a bit o' strike, mate?*
strip cell	place where staff can strip a prisoner (e.g. cooler, ice-box, padded cell)
strip search	intimate search on a prisoner in his cell – he is required to squat and show the soles of his feet (no female officer must be present)
stripes	see **E man**
strong box	special cell for unruly prisoner
stumpy	prisoner who has had his fingers taken off after having them crushed in a cell door
swinging the line	means of passing contraband from cell to cell by using a line

swoop	cigarette ends picked up by a prisoner, then broken up and packed into a pouch and sold on to heavy smokers
swooper	prisoner who picks up cigarette ends

T

TC	Therapeutic Community
tailor made	factory cigarette
tally	cell indicator to call a prison officer
tea's up	see **scran's up**
therapeuton	prisoner who talks in a therapeutic language (usually on coursework)
three'd up	three prisoners sharing a cell (originally done to deter homosexual acts)
tooled up	carrying a weapon
topped himself	committed suicide

topping shed	execution chamber (no longer used)
trusty	prisoner who is in a trusted job
turnkey	old-fashioned name for a prison officer (still used occasionally)
turn over	cell search
two'd up	two prisoners sharing a cell
two stretch	two years imprisonment

V

VC	Visiting Committee (no longer in use)
VDT	Voluntary Drug Test (usually once a month)
VP	Vulnerable Prisoner
VPU	Vulnerable Prisoners Unit
vet	prison doctor
visits	social visits from friends and relatives

W

wandering down the cut	sex with another prisoner
walkways	gangways on accommodation floor levels
wallflower	prisoner who talks of nothing else but escape
warden, the	prison governor
warder	prison officer
wellington boot	see **rubber socks**
whizz	drugs, usually speed
wing bike	homosexual who puts himself about in a sexual manner
wing bookie	prisoner who runs a betting book
wings	accommodation blocks
wired up	to connect a radio into the electric light circuit

wobbler		prisoner who has an outburst of anger, e.g. *he's throwing a wobbler*
wrong 'un		prisoner who can't be trusted

Y

YP	Young Prisoner
yard	exercise area

Z

zombie	prisoner on permanent medication
zooney suit	special shorts and skirt made of a strong fabric, worn only in a **strip cell**
zoot suit	special suit made of paper and worn by staff when attending a dirty protestor

OTHER TITLES AVAILABLE

Language Glossaries

American English/English American
Australian English/English Australian
Irish English/English Irish
Gay Slang
Geordie English
Lancashire English
Rhyming Cockney Slang
Scouse English
Yiddish English/English Yiddish
Scottish English/English Scottish
Yorkshire English
Ultimate Language of Flowers
Hip Hop English
Rude Rhyming Slang

History

The Death of Kings (A medical history
of the Kings & Queens of England)

Literary Quiz & Puzzle Books

Jane Austen
Brontë Sisters
Charles Dickens
Gilbert & Sullivan
Thomas Hardy
Sherlock Holmes
Shakespeare

All of these titles are available from good
booksellers or by contacting the publisher:
Abson Books London, 5 Sidney Square London
E1 2EY. Tel 020 7790 4737 Fax 020 7790 7346
email absonbooks@aol.com
web www.absonbooks.co.uk